HAPPY HOLIDAYS!

Hanukkah

by Pearl Markovics

Consultant:
Beth Gambro
Reading Specialist
Yorkville, Illinois

Contents

BEARPORT PUBLISHING

New York, New York

Hanukkah

What day is it?

It is Hanukkah!

It is Hanukkah.

I see the gifts.

It is Hanukkah.

I see the tops.

It is Hanukkah.

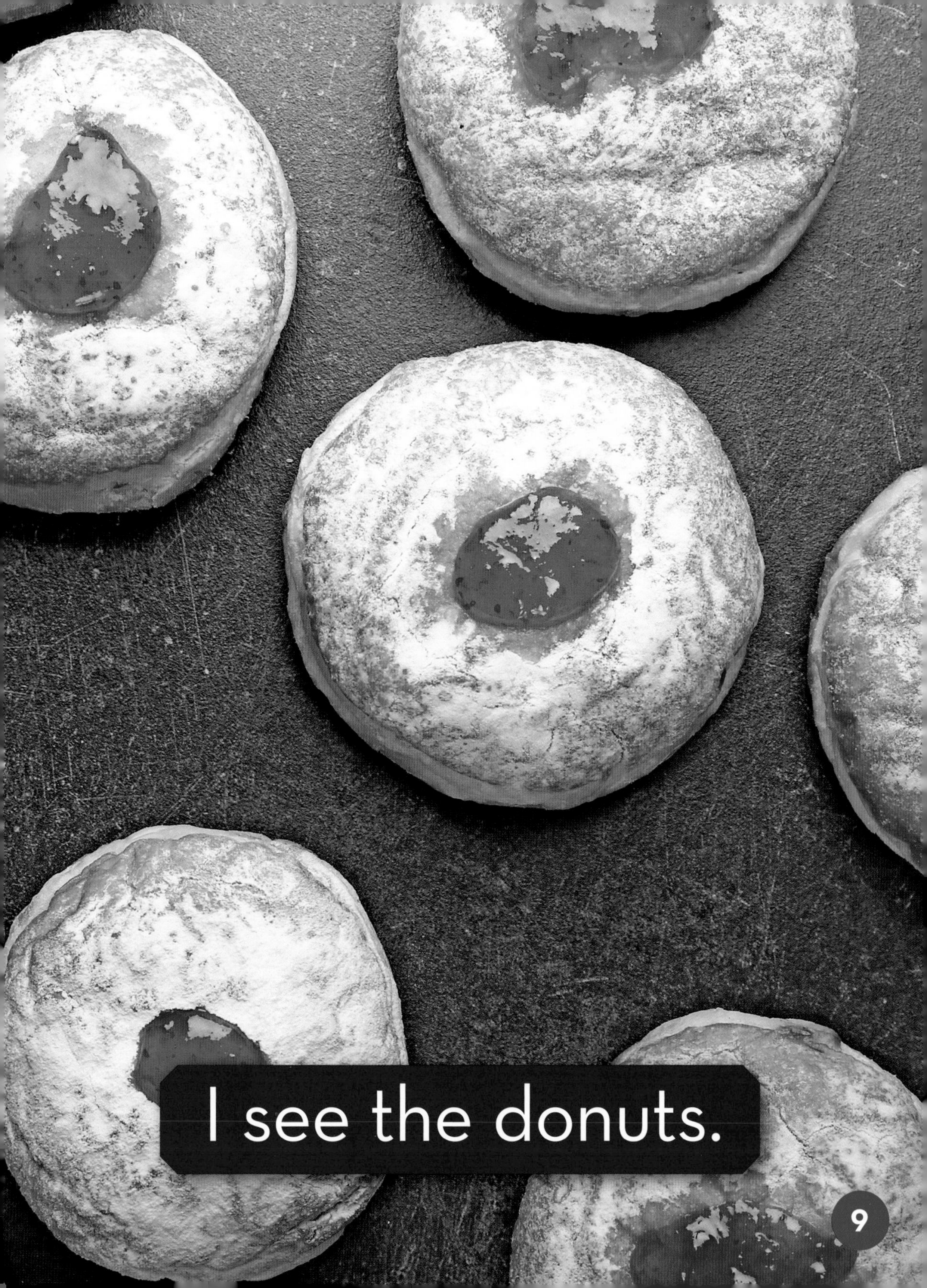

I see the donuts.

It is Hanukkah.

I see the candy.

It is Hanukkah.

I see the candles.

It is Hanukkah.

What do you see?

Key Words

candles

candy

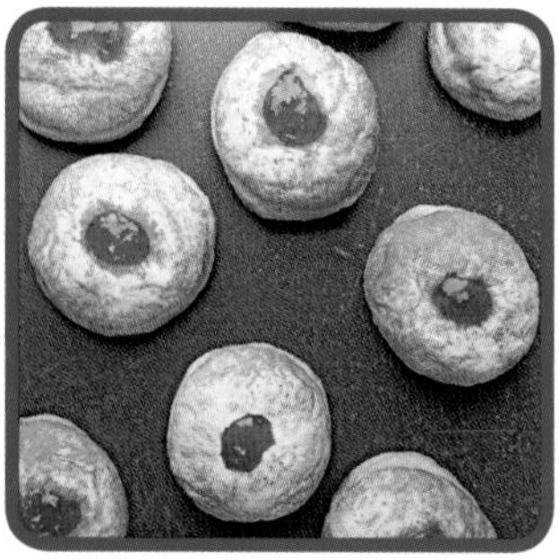

donuts

gifts

tops

Index

About the Author

Pearl Markovics loves holidays of every kind—especially the ones that include sweets and lots of presents.

Teaching Tips

Before Reading

- ✔ Guide readers on a "picture walk" through the text by asking them to name the things shown.
- ✔ Discuss book structure by showing children where text will appear consistently on pages.
- ✔ Highlight the supportive pattern of the book. Note the consistent number of sentences and words found on each page.

During Reading

- ✔ Encoursage children to "read with your finger" and point to each word as it is read. Stop periodically to ask readers to point to a specific word in the text.
- ✔ Reading strategies: When encountering unknown words, prompt readers with encouraging cues, such as:
    - **Does that word look like a word you already know?**
    - **It could be ___________, but look at ___________.**
    - **Check the picture.**

After Reading

- ✔ Write the key words on index cards.
    - **Have readers match them to pictures in the book.**
    - **Have children sort words by category (words that start with *c*, for example) or food type.**
- ✔ Encourage readers to talk about other holidays.
- ✔ Ask readers to identify their favorite page in the book. Have them read that page aloud.
- ✔ Ask children to write their own sentences about a holiday. Encourage them to use the same pattern found in the book as a model for their writing.

Credits: Cover, © Maglara/iStock; 1, © Mordechai Meiri/Shutterstock; 2–3, © elena_hramowa/iStock; 4–5, © christopherconrad/iStock and © tovfla/iStock; 6–7, © liza1979/Shutterstock; 8–9, © Africa Studio/Shutterstock; 10–11, © Silver Spiral Arts/Shutterstock, © Jovan Nikolic/Shutterstock, and © Rudmer Zwerver/Shutterstock; 12–13, © dra_schwartz/iStock; 14–15, © pushlama/iStock; 16T (L to R), © dra_schwartz/iStock, © Silver Spiral Arts/Shutterstock, © Jovan Nikolic/Shutterstock, and © Rudmer Zwerver/Shutterstock; 16B (L to R), © Africa Studio/Shutterstock, © christopherconrad/iStock, © tovfla/iStock, and © liza1979/Shutterstock.

Publisher: Kenn Goin **Senior Editor**: Joyce Tavolacci **Creative Director**: Spencer Brinker

Library of Congress Cataloging-in-Publication Data in process at time of publication (2019)
Library of Congress Control Number: 2018023629
ISBN-13: 978-1-64280-114-9 (library binding) | ISBN-13: 978-1-64280-149-1 (paperback)

10 9 8 7 6 5 4 3 2 1